WHEN I BECAME LIGHT

WHEN I BECAME LIGHT

A CONFIDENCE JOURNEY

Ilana Weinstein

NEW DEGREE PRESS

WHEN I BECAME LIGHT
A Confidence Journey

ISBN   979-8-88926-603-7 *Paperback*
          979-8-88926-602-0 *Ebook*

For Mom, Dad, Dana, Nanny, and Grandpa

In loving memory of Teri Weinstein and Norman Green

CONTENTS

———

A NOTE FROM
THE AUTHOR

A friend once told me my superpower is sunshine.
And I quite liked that, being a beacon for myself,
so I turned myself to light.

Except turning myself to light... took about ten years.

I joke with closest family and friends (which now includes you—welcome!) that my awkward phase lasted until I was twenty-five, or that I could make a very convincing case I'm still in it. Perhaps that is because I am verbose and derive a somewhat twisted enjoyment from being intentionally contrarian. Perhaps it is because, for a long time, I thought I'd never exit my awkward phase. Like a caterpillar to a butterfly—except I was convinced I'd just remain some lost squirming goo for all eternity.

As I navigated my teenage years, entered my twenties, and began to precariously take on adulthood, the world around me began to treat me as though my coming of age had happened and I should know how everything works now. It started to feel like I should be the most confident version of myself, know exactly what I wanted to do professionally, be in a happy and committed relationship headed toward marriage, and know when, exactly, I was going to give up on my fascination with New York City and move back to the suburbs like everyone else.

Instead, the picture looked quite different. I moved to New York City in 2012 to push my boundaries and become someone I was proud of, but she was (read: *is*) a work in progress. A committed relationship was buried beneath mountains of self-doubt and bad dates because I was not confident enough to tackle the land of dating as my whole and authentic self. Confidence, self-worth, and conviction in who I am and what my voice is has proven to be the highest of all the hurdles.

I write this note to you, as my proudly whole and authentic self!

At the time of writing this book, I will have lived in New York for about ten years. I love it and am never leaving, which is a statement that took me a very long time to be comfortable saying. This is probably because I was taught people think its cooler to hate on things than love them, but I digress.

Another joke I frequently make about the city I love is that New York City is the island of misfit toys. Because I live somewhere in which belonging is truly undefined, part of carving it out for myself was defining my own sense of worthiness and belonging, and what that looks like just for me.

What I needed was to let out my inner light—who I am, all my thoughts and opinions and feelings and ways of being—out into the world in the rawest of ways. My poetry was always a safe place to put my feelings. This book of my poetry is a dream realized, and is one of the steps in that journey. I'm not going to say it's the end, because I imagine there is no end to a confidence journey. There is a beginning though, and I am so happy that you'll get to see some of that in this book.

I don't know when I exactly decided "coming of age" was a time-bound thing. Or that there was a "right" way to do it, and if you were not on that path, something was wrong with your journey. While many of my girlfriends were dating seriously and getting engaged, I was spending my days attempting internet dating, working on how I viewed myself with my therapist, running around the outer boroughs of New York City eating noodles in every form, writing poems on the subway, and taking altogether too many dance classes per week.

No one celebrates that. We do not celebrate bringing your authentic self outside into the world every morning. We don't celebrate finding your art. We do not celebrate learning and accepting things about yourself. We don't celebrate loving where you live and the magic you find in every corner of your home, wherever that is for you. And we should.

It's not beautiful every second of the journey. Actually, to be honest, sometimes it's very awful, in every sense of the word. Sometimes, your journey is shaped and sized differently. Your light just might be taking a little longer. When you find it, it'll shine ten million times brighter. That is worth celebrating.

The book you're holding was written over the past ten years. It explores loneliness, intimacy, introspection, platonic and romantic love, and everything in between. No one ever told me how incredibly gratifying and beautiful it can be to grow. Since no one ever told me, I am here to tell you.

If you've ever questioned your power, your voice, your feelings—keep reading. If you've ever felt like life is coming at you too fast and somehow you're behind—keep reading (also, you're exactly where you're supposed to be!). If letting your light out is looking a little weird right now, I can promise you the weirdest lights shine the brightest.

This book celebrates an ongoing journey to self-worth and celebration. Every journey is the making of the most beautiful poem.

I am a poem worth reading

and so are you.

PART I

In the Beginning

I wore never being in love
like a Scarlet Letter,
I wore never having been loved
like makeup.
I wore strength
like a costume,
I wore loneliness
like a cloak.

And my sunshine was a brooch.
Brought out only sometimes
for special occasions
when I wanted to feel fancy.

The First Time

I cried barefoot in the driveway, standing on my tiptoes so
I could kiss you goodnight. Through the sticky July air, my
arms wrapped over your neck, my calves stretched tight

it was there that you told me you loved me.

Commute

When I look up
on my walk
up 7th Avenue to work,
I count office windows.
Roll my fingertips over
crumbling bricks,
stare through
the endless scaffolding,
and try my best
to practice
taking
just a moment
for the vast,
uninterrupted
expanse of the
Tuesday morning sky.

Visiting Birkenau, 2017

Shackle-free
on ancient tracks,
I walked out,
not looking back.
It was the first time I was
empowered,
the first time I knew
to be free,
a reminder I needed
was granted to me.

Forest Hills

I only know one way
to get to Manhattan.
The M or the R,
or the E or the F.
Or the bus, but I
don't know where it leaves me.
So does that make it one way,
two ways,
four ways,
or five?

No one moves to Forest Hills;
the neighborhood is old.
Old buildings,
old money,
old ladies
who remember the one time
you showed up
to the earlier spin class on a Sunday,
and then question you every time
you pass by on the way to the later one,
asking where you've been.

On an eighty-degree day in April,
I amble into the subway station
the way some people amble to a car
parked in their driveway.
I amble like the people who live here
and grow old here,

and know there's definitely
more than one way to get to Manhattan.

My Living Room

There is a spot
in my living room,
now home to
a new blue couch,
that once was bare.

It was there we danced
on New Year's Eve
to a Mariah Carey song
that always made me cry.
We stuck our socked feet
to the old wooden floor
and swayed like
December palm trees,
rooted but light.

I've spent my whole life
dancing;
but never before
and never again
with you.

January Snowstorm

When it snows
in New York City,
the flakes
a powdered sugar rain
unnecessary, yet
the sweetest of additions
quiet the city noise.
No subway growl,
no car horns,
only booted footsteps
or nothing.

The white weighted blanket
quiets the racing minds
of New Yorkers too.
Marveling in a living
souvenir snow globe
does for me.
There is something so sweet
about fleeting peace.

The Vestibule

His cigarette smelled sweet,
the smoke weaved over
the rusted iron fence outside
my new apartment building's front door
through the cracks between the glass
while I waited for a delivery truck.

The leaves curled over the welcome mat,
exactly the way it smelled to drink
hot beer in the square in Krakow,
but on a Saturday afternoon
waiting for a delivery truck
in Queens.

Lonely

I lay
in bed
that night
staring
at the slivers of
light painted
across my
bedroom wall,
a mural
I wanted to glean
nothing from
tears dropping
off the
end of
my nose.
I dreamt of heart
so very full;
but there was
just me.

Butterfly Girl

Butterfly girl; iridescent wings.
But only if you look close enough.

Her presence is captivating
her laugh infectious,
it launches glitter into the air
and draws a map of the room at the party.

Catching a butterfly is futile.
Will you spend the rest of your days
trying to shake glitter
out of your sweaters?

If you catch me,
will you listen?

Or will you clip my wings?

Nothing less than love

I say,
"All things with love,"
I say,
"Love in all things."
As in love yourself
Nothing less than love for yourself.
And when I search for love,
as I do
and have
and wished for
and wanted
for what feels like a lifetime
without love
No settling for the sake of love
But holding on for
Nothing less than love.

Giggles

A man on a street in San Francisco
wrote me a poem.
This sign taped to the table
where he sat said
"Give me a topic.
I'll write you a poem."
I gave him "cities."

I consider myself a collector, of sorts.
His dirty fingers dusted black
with soot from a day on the street
bounced along his typewriter
I stood alone to the side
giggling at my find,
a laugh I felt
floating around me like feathers
with each stroke of his old keys.

When he was done he read it.
He'd picked four cities and described their light,
I'd been to three of the four
and he'd been to only one but
the way he described the lights made it sound like
they too were giggling.

Returning to New York City

Tail beams form a map
Endless cars touch the skyline
as if to say "go."

Our First and Only Date

"I want a man who wears his heart on his sleeve,"
I said eagerly, on our first date
from a bench on the east side of Manhattan
at twilight,
looking out at Queens.

I thought this might be that man,
the one I've wished for
sitting next to me.
No one from the internet cesspool,
dirtier than the East River water,
had ever shown me their heart before.

"Don't stop wearing it.
Vulnerability is magic."
And it never goes out of style.

Soup Dumpling Love

I want love like soup dumplings.
Hold it with chopsticks,
Tongs
A spoon
Your fingers
Who cares.
Pick your favorite way
to get to the broth,
the best part,
slurping encouraged.
Wrapping stuck to your lips.
Swallow it nearly whole.
Go for another.
Order more than one steamer
kind of love.

Spin Class

The oldest rider
in Sunday morning spin class
has dozens of gold
bracelets jingling
from her delicate elbows
to her relaxed wrists,
which she shows off
when she enters the studio
to the young woman
on the spin bike next to her
in the back of the class
where she sits every week.

As class begins,
the riders begin grinding away.
The music blares,
the instructor gives commands.
She unrolls the local newspaper
across her handlebars
and pedals in slow motion,
cycling through
wildflower honey
in no particular hurry.

To my someone, someday

I wish
on every loose eyelash,
11:11, and coin tossed in a fountain
for you and I
to find each other.

I think people should know
how badly
their presence is wanted.

But most of all,
I wish
I get to tell you that someday.

Dream House

"If you didn't live in New York,"
my coworker asks me,
over our second and third beers
at a loud Friday happy hour,
"where would you live?"

"The beach," I tell her,
without a breath between my words
"I'd live by the beach
in a house on stilts
with big windows.

Close enough
to the shore that I
could fall asleep
to the sound of
the waves pulling sand
from the beach
instead of
a window AC unit,
and close enough to smell
the salt in the air
first thing in the morning
before coffee.
Somewhere
I could watch the sunrise."

I draw a sip from the top of my glass.
"But only with someone I love;
I would never do it alone."

Platonic Love in Pittsburgh

It was on the overnight bus
home to New York City
after a weekend
exploring Pittsburgh
that I realized it was love.
Eight hour bus rides
across rural Pennsylvania
are really good for deciding how you feel.

It's breakfast in silence.
No need to fill space.
One word answers to questions
cackling in the backseat of the Uber
Forcing each other to drink water
after steins of beer downtown
Never caring who
was actually the third wheel.

It was love I found
the Saturday night we spent
dancing in the doorway of the bar
waiting for our ride home.

The Worst Date I've Ever Been On

The worst date I have ever been on
was with a boy named James.
I do not call him a man
but a boy.
He does not deserve
to be called a man.

The boy and I
went to a speakeasy in the East Village.
A hidden door behind a barber shop
Dim lighting,
black ceiling,
marble bar.
Overpriced cocktails,
overdressed patrons,
a disco ball.

It was the first time
I'd ever been on a cocktail bar date.
He bought all my drinks.
A gentleman,
or so I thought.
Until he started telling me
how close we were to his place.

I told him no.
He told me
it was not an ask, but
an expectation.

The date quickly devolved
into a corner dive bar
serving dirt cheap beers.
I told him to go fuck himself
and got in a yellow cab home.

That was last time I ever let myself go
on a very bad date
ever again.

PART II

My Coping Mechanism for Lots of Things

You're not acting
like somebody that I know.
So now
I am going to
write you
into somebody that I do.

Inside Jokes

Instagram tells me
my behavior indicates of deep loneliness.
For every internet user these days is also a scientist.

At my first job my coworker had a sticker
on her laptop that read "You ≠ user"
Which is supposed to be a saying that is only funny
if you do one kind of job for a living
but is not chuckle-worthy otherwise

Because if you did chuckle but you didn't understand why,
she would look at you funny and then explain it to you
Which is how all inside jokes are ultimately ruined.

The internet is lots of laptop stickers
you only understand
if you're in on the joke.
There's no science to jokes.
And I am not in on a lot of jokes,
so I make up my own
about being lonely.

Today I Started Therapy Again

"I'm a well-adjusted adult,"
I lie to the therapist over the phone.
Except these days it seems
anxiety's just keeping me alone.

My confidence is in reverse,
a train on the wrong tracks.
No longer can I even pretend
to ignore all the things I lack.

All I want of this restart
is for my little heart
to be ready for and worthy of
its missing part.

Signs of Wear

At home in the bookcase under the TV
are my poetry books,
all with dog-eared pages.

People visit, take them off the shelves,
and gasp in horror that the books
are snuggled against each other
and the creases,
they are permanent.

I ripped a hole in one of the covers.
The neon green one with the thickest spine
I'd been carrying it around in my backpack for weeks
Tossed my keys in at just the wrong angle
to puncture the softcover.
I noticed it when I finished reading it.
The tiniest bit of light through to the cover page

There is something poetic about that too.

Dancing in Public

When there is music
suddenly
every vein in my body
is unable to carry blood with ease.
As if to keep my body working
I must move
to the thumping bass
of whatever is playing.

If I know steps to a song
it's worse.
My hands and arms
swoop and swipe
to a pattern of movement they know,
regardless of who or what
is in front of them
if they are threaded through the straps
of my backpack
or clutching tightly to
the handles of a gift bag.

My feet work best
when they are tapping.
When my big toes
are taking turns
keeping beat.
When they are shuffle-ball-changing
across train platforms
around strollers,

dodging arms
laden with grocery bags,
hands gripping
dripping umbrellas.

When there is music,
it doesn't matter
if it is from
department store speakers
a booming car radio,
a street performer,
inside my head.

When I am dancing,
it doesn't matter who's watching.

A Global Pandemic Realization

It is my eightieth walk
of the hundred days of quarantine
in my hometown
where nothing changes,
when I finally admit
to my best friend of twenty years
that I don't wish to be alone.

I used to tell myself
I wished to be alone.
When really,
my very biggest fear
was ending up alone.
I cried frequently
about being alone,
often alone,
because I am the only one I know
who is alone
and does not want to be alone.
And that
is the loneliest part of it all.

Crying about being single, again

"Sometimes,"
I choke out,
on my bi-weekly phone call
with my therapist,
the screen of
my iPhone
sticking to my cheek,
in full tears,
like our last session.

"Sometimes I wonder if
I haven't been
a good enough
person
to have
my person."
It's a thing I've said to her
every phone call
just about every which way I could.
Every way except
to fix it.

And my therapist
says:
"We're just going to
throw that out
right now.
In this universe,

that's just
not true."

I hope one day
I believe her.

Not Manhattan Summer

There's nothing I love more
than the speed at which the commuter trains
rocket through the rail station
in my old neighborhood.
They fly so fast
they rattle the brick train platform
the electric rails
sparklers

or
the way the mid-summer air smells
in the outer boroughs of the city
— a cologne of tar, beer,
the East River, sunscreen,
empanadas and meat on a stick,
resilient grass fighting
the endless pounding of human steps,
sweat.

The scent lingers
for almost as long
as it takes for the trains
to keep flying East.

Poet's Eye

Look at me for too
long, and you just might become
yourself, a poem

Where to See the Sunset

I want to bottle the feeling
of walking to the G train,
knowing it'll take me
to my new favorite neighborhood,
Greenpoint,
where the sunsets are kept.

I am a sunset girl.
No, I am not comparing myself to one.
Every sunset is my first.
If there is a layer of sky that is pink,
I become five years old again.
I talk about how
my ballerina tutu matches the sky.
If there is orange I count
the skyscraper mirrors turned creamsicle.

See the sunset with me and
I turn to rainwater through your fingers.
Just like the time
the fireworks on the river
came too close on the 4th of July
and we thought
we might walk home with
yellow light in our pockets.

Light we could paint the sky with
again tomorrow.

My Therapist's Valuation of Our Bi-weekly Phone Calls

"You are building
the strongest foundation
and one day,
all the finishing touches
will make it
perfect."

Post-Pandemic New York

One Friday in September
I ate breakfast on the steps
of the Met, like I was in *Gossip Girl*.

My city was new again that day.
Like autumn in Berlin
two years ago.
The thrill of new sidewalks to dance on,
a city melody,
voluminous and loud,
that was unfamiliar.
The scent of fall leaves before they disappear
for the season.

That Friday in September,
the Manhattan blocks
pulsated;
sizzled.
The air tasted sweet and crisp
and smelled of hope,
fall leaves before they disappear
for the season, and
sidewalks begging
to be danced upon again.

Self-Actualizing While Having COVID-19

After days on the couch
too fatigued to do much else
other than think,
I declared
the job is not the dream
and there was so much more
space.

Suddenly,
there was reading before bed
with a steaming mug of tea.
Piles of books
on every table in the apartment.
Fragmented poems
in a Notes app,
in email,
after work,
just about anywhere.

A messy artist
moved in.
Or,
she lived in the space
for the first time.
She never knew such a small space
could hold so much joy.

A Man I Never Expected to Fall For, and Some Other Stuff I Never Said

When Molly handed me her phone
over a picnic blanket piled high
with emptied craft beer cans
and White Claws,
I saw your face again.

The first thing I thought
(but did not say)
was *"Oh wow, he got cute."*

I knew you at fourteen.
All dyed pink hair
and a mullet cut,
dirty sneakers,
black T-shirts
of bands no one knew.

In the early days of May
we are sharing fried snacks and catching up
in the biergarten behind the pub
on Queens Boulevard on a weeknight.
I am unsurprised to find
you still listen to bands
that absolutely no one knows.
I am surprised to find
I think you have the prettiest hazel eyes
in the whole wide world.

Just before the 4th of July
we went to Soho.
I was a pat of butter in a hot pan over
the peach Jordan Mids you helped me find
next to your beat-up classic ones.
His & hers
Holding the tail of your red raincoat
up the subway stairs.
Falling asleep on your shoulder
on the G train,
headed home.
That was the day I let myself fall.
I never told anyone that, either.

Another few weeks and
we get pasta for dinner again, a thing for us.
Us.
I love the way it sounds.
I have always wished for someone to be us with.
Afterward we watch the sun dive behind the
black Manhattan skyline
and I am resisting the urge to crawl
right into your lap and arms
because it is the hottest day of August
but also because
I don't want to know how you feel.
Not during sunset.

And when I finally did ask you,
Do you want to do this?
Days later
the answer was, as I had feared,

as it always is,
no.

And here's another thing I never said:
I swallowed
one gigantic pill
curing me of the things
I didn't say and
said I'd never do,
and then I wished really hard
for it to be you.

The Power of Loneliness

The universe asks, with a smirk,
'Can you sit in your loneliness?'
And then tells you it's wrong if you do.
So I say to the universe,
"I am not afraid to show you my loneliness anymore."

It's my favorite flannel,
the one I stole from my dad's closet years ago,
kept as "house clothes,"
worn outside.
A baby French press,
a splash of oat milk,
a single serving.
A Saturday full of nowhere to be.
All dressed up for dinner
with an empty chair;
people watching as
the best company.
There is no shame in dessert,
all the flavored layers of sunset
just me and the twilight breeze.

I switched my Scarlet Letter for
a bustier wrapped in diamonds
so I can wear the city lights I wrote poems about,
so they reflect on titanium walls
and storefront windows.
Not because diamonds are a girl's best friend,
but because I
have learned to be my own best friend.

I wear my loneliness
like the superhero cape it is.
I'll tell you what color it is for the day
every morning
even if you didn't ask.

Friend-Zoned

Some days,
it is really hard to be
just another one of your friends.
I don't want to be
just another one of your friends.
I want to be your girl.

But I know to keep you
I don't get to be your girl.
We get to be just friends.
And I'll do it but
some days are harder than others.
Today is one of them.

I don't want to be your friend today.

PART III

A Poem Worth Reading

A friend once told me my superpower is sunshine.
And I quite liked that, being a beacon for myself,
so I turned myself to light.
Lifted all the heavy thoughts
into pages of art.

I have always known that I am different.
So when I became light
I cut my hair and
let the curls go whatever direction they pleased.
Painted my butterfly wings opaque
So you couldn't miss them
Grew wildflowers from my palms
Did not apologize for using windows as my mirror
on the subway on the way to Brooklyn
Wore my sneakers every day this week.

I am not shy.
Not so much that I
will hold conversation with
the bare walls of my apartment until
they brim with color,
But shy enough, that at the party
I will take myself out to the front stoop
and listen to the sounds of my thoughts over
chatter,
the cars rolling over the bridge across the river,
the clatter of bicycle chains,
the footsteps of the hipsters bar-hopping,

and I'll photosynthesize
in city lights.

When I became light
I made my words louder.
I know in my heart I am poetry.
But I have always wondered what kind?
Am I the kind people flip past quickly
as they read poetry books in coffee shops
because they do not understand?
Or am I the one the eighth graders dissect for their litera-
ture classes,
so many times over that now
there is little meaning left to look for at all?
Or am I the kind you give to someone you love
attached to a bouquet of flowers?

I may never know.
But I do know
I am a poem worth reading.

Holding Pattern

Waiting on
Everything.
The other shoe
to drop at work.
Whether or not
a big dream will
materialize.
Another new job,
the third in three years.
The return of dance class,
weekly
if I'm lucky.
I'll settle for a few sacred steps
anytime, though.

A new apartment,
hopefully one with
big bright windows.

Just the right pot
for a very
complicated houseplant.

Mundane Friday Morning Work from Home Fantasies

In my favorite fantasy,
it is Friday morning.
We are together
"working" in the basement
of the Brooklyn apartment
you love so much,
and by "working" I mean
we are still in our pajamas
drinking coffee
and having a conversation
that's changed directions so many times
that even we don't quite know where it started
like every conversation we've ever had.

In my favorite fantasy,
I tiptoe up to the back of your desk chair
behind your soaring wall of records
and appear.
We are talking and I
am twirling about in my underwear
and one of your band T-shirts
Which is not to say that
twirling about in my underwear
is not a thing that
does not happen in real life,
there just isn't an audience.

Ode to the Blue Couch

The blue couch
has been in my apartment for four years.

It was where I spent many a day
when the world was shut down,
curled up watching *Harry Potter*
over and over again.

It has cradled the heads of my friends,
of my sweetly sleeping sister,
of anyone needing to catch a flight
out of Kennedy or LaGuardia.
I keep finding crumbs between its cushions
most of pink salt popcorn
every time I have a guest.

It's my favorite place to cry.
Belly down with
one of the wide pillows
under my face and chest.
I always pretend it is the embrace
of someone who loves me.
I dig my always short nails
into the faux velvet
and pretend it is
a cotton T-shirt
of a band I don't know
or a show I've never watched
or a Kirkland one that belongs to my mother.

I don't know if my imagination saves me
or makes me cry harder,
though I imagine both.

I am moving in three weeks.
Everything in the apartment is going.
The pillows are getting brand new covers,
but the couch
is coming with me.

November Sundays

One Sunday
I stood on the corner of Mott St.
and watched the stream of
cars and bicycles combine
to one rushing river,
and I wondered
if the tourists found Sunday afternoon
as charming as I did.

Sunday is underrated.
The dusky daybreak tastes
of sleeping in.
The biting wind
loosens my curls.
Near-winter light makes
the buildings
and the streetlights
glow pink.
I think it's how
the universe apologizes
for new darkness
before dinner.

I accept it because
pink
is my most favorite color.

Everything in New York City Happens Fast

I talked about moving
every day for a year.
My friend Anthony from down the street
heard about it
over and over again
until suddenly, one week in December,
I was moving in 10 days.

What I really wanted was
more time to sit in the change.
To ride the scary building elevator
one more time,
before I trade it in
for four flights of marble stairs.
To have one last dance party of one
in the basement laundry room.
Or one more ice cream for dinner
at the old ice cream shop on Metropolitan.
Not like I couldn't have it ever again in the future,
but now
it would no longer be convenient.
And in New York,
inconvenience
is the utmost deterrent.

In New York, everything happens fast.
Unless, of course,
you need something fixed

like a leak over your kitchen cabinets.
And then the task is arduous,
but everything else is fast.

Especially goodbyes.

A Thank You Note to My First New York Apartment

68th Road,
Thank you for 4 years.

For 3 jobs,
1 master's degree,
1 boyfriend,
1 breakup,
a 25th birthday party.

For quite a few sleepovers
a sink backup,
a laundry room fire,
several very bad dates,
dozens of post-dance protein smoothies.

For enduring watermelon juice
and laundry detergent
on the carpet,
Moroccan mint tea on
the couch pillows,
an over-shaken Sapporo
all over the kitchen table,
a bathroom ceiling leak.

For giving me
an unpoetic desensitization
to the tub-shower
always back-filling.
Countless laughs,

considerable tears,
and 1 global pandemic.

So much finding myself
happened inside your four peeling walls.
No amount of paint will ever change that.

Remembering to Leave Things Behind

On my last day in the old apartment,
I slept with the window
next to the fire escape open.
My upstairs neighbors
took the window AC unit that morning
which did nothing to let in more starlight
and everything
to let in the December night air.
I hoped it would help me sleep.
Hoped it would blow away
the sawdust from my hair.

And just maybe it would blow away
all the lingering doubt.
Just far enough away that I might
forget to look for it.
Forget to pack it in a moving box.
Forget to take it with me.

I Might've Fallen in Love and Now I Don't Know What to Do with It

I don't know the emotion
that was left the morning after
we put the new bookcase together
and drank tall boys of Allagash White on a Monday
and talked about other people's weddings.

I woke up like
I had just run a marathon,
crushing weight
over my neck and chest,
yet
I wanted to dance.

The apartment felt bigger
And also emptier.
You do not live here and
we moved every last piece of furniture around.
What do you call that feeling?

My Artist Imposter Syndrome

Forgive me for what I'm about to tell you
Might sound just plain sappy
I've relinquished being a "brooding poet"
It turns out,
I write even better poems happy.

What a Fourth Floor Walkup Taught Me

In the battle of small stubborn woman
versus big brown shipping box,
the marble stairs will always win.

Laundry is so much more satisfying
when it involves you walking up and down,
up and down,
with detergent bottles on each arm
and your keys
woven through your fingers.

You must earn your takeout
by retrieving it yourself from the delivery man.
He biked here in the windy twilight
and will likely refuse to walk
the four flights up
because his night has just started.

The bed frame that shipped
in two monstrous pieces
must be sliced opened in the vestibule
and marched up the stairs
by an army of two
piece by piece
to the unfinished bedroom for assembly.
But first,
you'll probably need to rest and catch your breath.

And you will sleep on the floor
with your mattress on a box spring
until you learn the apartment,
like so many other things,
will not come together
all at once.

PART IV

On Becoming Unstubborn

Stubbornness is a cool leather jacket.
Sharp silver zippers,
hardware that reverberates when I walk
You must earn the right to wear such armor.
I walk like I want people to know I earned that.
I talk like I want people to know it too.

Until one day I realized
my stubborn soul was keeping me from love.
I walked like I wanted no one beside me,
talked like there was only space for me.
So I wore my leather jacket in the December rain
in hopes it would melt the armor away.

Instead I was soaked to the bone and
all ten toes turned to ice.
I had to stand in the shower
face to the scalding water
just to warm up.
I was wrong about how quickly I said I would change;
it was chattering teeth and numb fingertips
for weeks.

One sunny morning,
I awoke to find a softened jacket
slung over the back of my kitchen chair.
The zipper dulled, the corners gentler,
buttery leather under dry-skinned hands.
The hardware still clattering, but softer

against the wrist of
another unstubborn soul
in a cool leather jacket.

A Brooklyn Love Story

My grandparents fell in love in Brooklyn.
I was thinking of them
under bright blue Thursday skies,
bright blue like my grandfather's eyes;
and lipstick-kiss clouds,
as a busker band played blues
in McCarren Park,
and February in New York City
was not really blue for the day.

I find myself in Brooklyn often.
I discovered a spot on Manhattan Avenue
that sounds like Hungary,
songs of consonants;
and smells like Paris,
coffee and smoke.
My grandmother always told us
she'd never smoked
even though we knew she did,
and she'd regale elaborate tales
of a childhood spent in Budapest,
even though she was born here.
Williamsburg was where she grew up and I
think she'd be quite the hipster herself—
all bold makeup and opinions,
keeping things to herself in the name of irony—
if she were still here.
My grandfather was a Brooklyn boy too.
He loved everything he knew about her.

When I come to Brooklyn
I picture their first meeting
dancing in a parking lot sockhop
in Sheepshead Bay,
but today,
their meeting looks like swaying
to the busker band
under bright blue skies and
lipstick-kiss clouds
in McCarren Park.

Mini Time Capsule

We went for dinner in my old neighborhood,
the first time back since I moved.
It was a little over a month since I
walked the back route to the dumpling place
we're all obsessed with.
The unassuming one on Austin Street,
best accessed by the path behind the middle school,
the one that turns into the
most incredible crimson canopy in the fall.

We have an unspoken truth
in New York City:
You'll stay longer
than your landmarks.
Places that become favorites to you
come and go as quickly as goodbyes,
and when they don't,
suddenly it feels like time
was shoved in a subway car
that is stuck in train traffic,
and for a moment
nothing moves.

A Magician Disguised as the Man I Am Dating

Before we went to bed the other night,
you told me to take a deep breath
because you were counting the decreasing seconds
between each inhale,
pulled me out of my own mind and
scooped me into your arms
and buried your face in my neck.

I think that your best trick is slowing down time
weeks have more weekends
days have more hours.

My hair smells like you all the time now.
It's tricky because when I turn my head
I think you will appear behind me.
It makes me miss you,
which feels dumb.
Not dumb for missing you;
I like to miss you.
Having someone to miss
means you have
someone special.

What I don't like is
what I'll miss
if you disappear.

How to Decorate a New Apartment

You decorate a new apartment
not with
the painting of a red teddy bear
in a beanie
purchased from an artist
in Boston,
nor
the collection of Metrocards
encased in glass knowing
they will soon slip into history.

You decorate by
arranging the clean dishes
in rainbow.
Singing to the plants;
creating their voices
so they sing back.
Your older cousins' laughter,
as they sit on the blue couch
across from one another,
their conversation fast and exciting
like the race cars they are telling you about.

I imagine my walls
pantries filled with giggling.
When the apartment is too quiet I ask them
to share their contents with me
and imagine all the people
I love in my living room,

too many of us for a New York apartment,
on every square inch of rug and floor,
filling back in
the balance of the wall banks.

Things I Should Know Better Than to Do as a New Yorker

I left the house in heeled booties
to take a long walk through Astoria
       Impractical shoes are a city cardinal sin.
to a coffee shop
to write poetry
       Like every other outer-borough artist, I know
only to find that you aren't allowed
to sit inside,
       COVID turned coffee shops into drive-thrus,
       the ones we left behind in the suburbs
so I purchased an iced coffee because
it felt weird to leave empty-handed and
went back out into the winter
and walked all the way home.
       I am too proud to own that my shoes were wrong
       and that it's too cold to walk.

Contemplating My Existence on a Monday

My best friend from college texts me
on a Monday night.
I am in the Queens Plaza subway station,
impatiently awaiting the next E train,
so I can hop another at Court Square
to spend the night in Brooklyn,
snuggled with a new other half
a term I love to use,
and one I am also afraid of.

A video appears.
A little scruffy Yorkie and her toy,
about the same size,
on a rug I've definitely slept on before
after a 23rd birthday party that got out of hand.

It is then I realize we have grown up.
Three weeks ago she bought me
celebratory "new apartment" flowers.
I was trimming them at my kitchen sink
shocked that I have somehow managed to keep them
blooming and alive.

Now, there are things that need
all of our beings to survive:
professions,
partnerships,
puppies.

The thought that one day she will call me
and it will be a ring on her left hand,
the kind she always wished for.
Maybe one day I will call her
to show her mine too,
a thing I never even dreamt I would say;
something I am afraid of too.

Sleeping on the rug feels so ancient
I should be studying it in a textbook.
The kind we shared in college
because textbooks were expensive
and sharing was more fun.

We share moments now.
They keep getting bigger,
scarier,
more permanent.
I'm almost certain
I like sharing those even better.

A List of Things It'll Never Be the Right Time to Tell You

I can't wait to wake up
next to you
on Saturday morning.

I'm not ready.

I want you to be it for me.

I wished 1000 wishes for you.

How will I know when to say, "I love you?"

Parting with who I was before you feels like death
and also rebirth.

I hang on every word you say to me. Please be careful with
that.

You're beautiful.

I thought I'd absolutely hate
hearing you call me "Baby"
But I don't,
I actually love it.

I can't believe you happened.

I love being yours.

The Cool New Yorker I Always Wanted to Be

The family visiting from Europe asks me where Times
Square is.
They're lost on their way to Midtown.
They've found me on my lunch break in the park,
escaping the office.

At eighteen I moved to Manhattan,
a place I'd come to only as a girl
to glittered sidewalks and theater marquees.
All I wanted was to shop in old bookstores
Have a local bar that knew me by name
or a coffee shop, I wasn't picky,
as long as my beverage waited for me.

I wished to walk the same dance studios halls
as the Broadway stars.
Imagined how wonderful it would feel
to never have to consult Google Maps
to know exactly which exit of the subway train
was closest to my destination.
Not because suddenly
I'd developed a passion for cardinal directions,
but because I'd just know.

It's ten years since I first moved to New York.
I left Manhattan and moved to Queens and became
one of those girls.
Those girls who talk about
the outer boroughs and their magic,

gentrification,
dollar pork buns,
and they write poetry about it.
The only coffee shop that ever knew my order
was the Dunkin' by my college dorm.
It would be years before I'd spot someone from
my favorite Broadway show
spinning tip-toed on sneakers in the front row of
a sold-out Midtown dance class.
It turns out they aren't as nice as I hoped.
I still regularly consult Google Maps to this day.

But every once in a while,
I get out on the West side
of the 23rd St. stop,
or the North exit at 34th St.,
or get in the right subway car to get off
closest to the grocery store in Long Island City.
I don't even really think about it anymore,
my legs just know.
They carry me to the people I love,
to the places I'm happiest,
to a cup of coffee I ordered,
because the barista sees too many people in one day
to remember just mine.

And so I direct the lost family uptown,
to glittered sidewalks and theater marquees,
and they are endlessly impressed
I have consulted nothing.
And I realize, in a different way

I am the cool New Yorker
I always wanted to be.

Weddings

I never gave much thought to weddings.
At least, not before there was you.
I don't know anything about the shape of gowns,
or what bridesmaids are supposed to do.

White dresses, to me,
seem like they are asking for stains.
I can't tell you what to look for in a diamond.
And what do you do if on your day, it rains?

I remember the moment my oldest friend told me
she was sure she'd met him, "the one."
I was in the passenger seat of her orange car
in disbelief of finding him, like that, just done.

In two years I'll get to be in their wedding.
I can only imagine how beautiful she'll look.
When she talks of all the wedding plans,
it sounds like a fairytale out of a book.

It seemed like it might never be for me,
that easy, I mean to say.
After dozens of failed internet dates
I came to believe it'd stay that way.

That was before I knew there was you,
my person, my very own "the one."
Now we stand together in the steaming shower
and talk about our wedding, just for fun.

In My Corner of Queens

There is so much light
that the night sky
never darkens.
All nights
look like twilight
and the stars
are apartment windows.

My new building
is catty-corner
to a neighborhood taco spot.
The smell crests over the brick walls
of my new patio
and makes me hungry all of the time.
I think that makes me
a member of the family.

My new neighborhood
feels like the first day of school.
I don't know where anything is.
I need to find my homes,
places for all my things.
The coffee shop around the corner,
the one with the teal storefront on 34th Ave,
where I wrote this poem,
is the best start.

My new apartment
faces the railroad I take
to the house I grew up in.
When I take the train to my parents
I can point out my balcony through the window.
At night from my new bedroom,
I hear the blaring horn
of the "drunk train,"
the last one out of Penn Station,
slicing through the dulled buzzing
of Astoria at night
not quite as loud and endless
as Manhattan,
taking all the stragglers
home.

For the Love of Lazy Saturday Mornings

Mornings take on new meaning with you.
I never knew how much I liked
the slice of morning light that pours over your messy bed
through your blackout curtains
that don't really blackout your bedroom at all.
How much I'd enjoy
your neighbor's overweight gray cat
walking the rusted chain-link fence like a tightrope
or the birds chirping in the mulberry tree by the back door,
the one that stains the whole yard purple over the summer.
That I'd wait all week to wake up
with your stubbled face
burrowed under my chin.

You kiss me in your sleep.
It is only recently I discovered
you aren't awake when you talk to me at night.
Last night you told me I am your favorite person in
the world.
I don't ever sleep well in your bed
because it is not mine
and because I like being awake enough to hear you.

This Saturday morning, we stayed in bed
and sent your roommate out for iced coffees
in celebration of spring sunrises.
We ate dessert for breakfast
and danced in the kitchen.

Weekend mornings are longer with you.
We danced until it was well after noon.
I hold on to these mornings all week long,
until the next.

A Letter to My Seventeen-Year-Old Self

Dear Seventeen,

I think of you often.
I know you think
you might just eat lunch
alone on the windowsill
of your high school Spanish classroom forever,
but I can promise you
you won't.
I'm here to spill some secrets.

One day,
you'll just about die
over the closet you have.
And sometimes,
when you are bored
on a Tuesday night
with nowhere to go,
you'll play dress up
in your own clothes.

That closet is inside an apartment
in New York City
that is all yours.
In New York City,
you get to dance your heart out
every night of the week
or on the weekends
or basically any time you want.

I know Mom tells you no
to extra dance classes now.
You'll thank her for that one day.

You get to hold on
to some incredible,
beautiful
and special people from these years
you've so quickly wished away.
There's even a few who will surprise you.
You'll see they become
some of your most precious friends.

All those precious old friends of yours
will meet the loves of their lives.
You will meet them,
they will become a part of your life,
and you get to love them too.

There's also all the
incredible and wonderful people
you meet as an adult.
You'll find them in the unlikeliest of places.
They will become incredibly special to you too.

And not only that,
all of those people
love you for exactly who you are.
I know,
it sounds like it might never be.

You're going to grow up to be
someone you are so very proud of.

I can't wait for you to see.

All my love,
Twenty-Seven

ACKNOWLEDGMENTS

First and foremost, all my love and gratitude to Mom and Dad: The number one item on my bucket list completed, all because of you. Thank you for always encouraging me to go after my goals and dreams.

To Nanny, who has always been supportive of my art from day one.

And to my sister Dana, who has whole-heartedly believed in every crazy idea I've come up with, including this book.

To my friends: So many of you believed in me, in this book, and in my art before I believed in it myself. Without you all, I would've never gone through and finished this. All the messages, virtual cheers, actual cheers, the unwavering support, every "Tell me everything about the book!"—it all has meant so much.

Taylor Seckler, thank you for being a constant source of support, love, and light for me. You came into my life at exactly the right time, and for that I am forever grateful.

Monica Tan, you were the first person I told when I got into the Book Creators program. The fact that my poems will wear one of your concepts as their cover forever is so incredibly special.

Minh Anh Nguyen, Gab Sisino, Kelsey Price, and Drew Crocitto—I cannot believe you four read every single poem before we went to print. No amount of words will ever sufficiently explain how much the comments, thoughts, and ideas the four of you shared elevated this book.

Ali Carbone, I'm so glad we had that talk in your car on the way home after dance that night. Writing books was way more fun together!

Regina Stribling, this book's soul started with you. Working with you was freeing, transformative, and endless fun. I hope I have made you proud.

Eric Koester, Kehkashan Khalid, and everyone at the Creator Institute and New Degree Press, thank you for taking a chance on a girl with some old poems and a bucket list.

A special thank you to Sway Café in Astoria and Odd Fox Coffee in Greenpoint: Many of these poems were written, rewritten, and edited at your tables and with one of your coffees in hand.

And finally, to everyone who preordered a copy of *When I Became Light*, and for anyone who purchases a copy in the future: On behalf of present-day Ilana and teenage Ilana somewhere in the delicate fabric of space and time, thank you, from the bottom of my heart, for making my dream come true.

Enzo Badia

PJ Bracciodieta

Bianca Brigandi

Lisa Chi

Nicole Dash

Yash Desai

Sherry Finkel

Megan Fisher

Sam Giambrone

Anbar Hassan

Alexandra Kennedy

Eric Koester

Paula Lamendola

Emily Lawson

Liz Lombardi

Abe Martinian

Holly Bentley

Kendra Bradley

Ali Carbone

Drew Crocitto

Lisa DeAngelis

Melissa Escobar

Rian Finnegan

Julia Geisler

Barbara Green

Ryan Isabelle

Hanna Kim

Donna Krompinger

Courtney Lamendola

Morgan Leopold

Ian Mabie

Anthony Miguel

Kristy Millette

Tom Murray

Anh Nguyen

Minh-Anh Nguyen

Richard Park

Catharine Petroff

Billy Pittman

Kelsey Price

Elene Robakidze

Stephanie Roseti

Marianna Savoca

Taylor Seckler

Gabrielle Sisino

Johnny Snyder

Victoria Spinelli

Natalie Steinberg

Megan Mueller

Liane Ng

Dawn Nguyen

Lindsay Owen

Geri Pesko

Monica Pigeon

Sarah Porteous

Daniel Rice

Gabi Rogers

Julia Sanders

Kalli Schumacher

Jamie Seiden

Samantha Sloan

Jennifer Sovey

Amy Staub

Monica Tan

Claire Tran   Courtney Tulig

Nishanth Viswanath   Dana Weinstein

Paula Weinstein   Stan Weinstein

Steven Weinstein   Tobi Weinstein

Leann Werner   Deb White

Vanessa Wu   Jenny Yang

Jierui Zhao   Lenny Zhou

Ilana Weinstein is a very proud New Yorker. Though she holds two business degrees from Pace University and Binghamton University, she has always had a deep love of art. She wrote *When I Became Light* to chronicle her own coming of age in the city she loves most, in hopes of being the example she needed growing up, as she tackled (and continues to tackle) adulthood.

Ilana enjoys any dish involving noodles, dancing anywhere and everywhere, and spending time with her family and friends. She is passionate about all the little magical corners of the world, and will absolutely say "yes" if you ask her to watch a sunset. Ilana believes that poetry is for all to enjoy, and you can connect with her on LinkedIn, via email at poemsbyilana@gmail.com, or at @poemsbyilana on Instagram.